Gemini
Astrology Coloring Book

Color Your Zodiac Sign

The 12 Signs

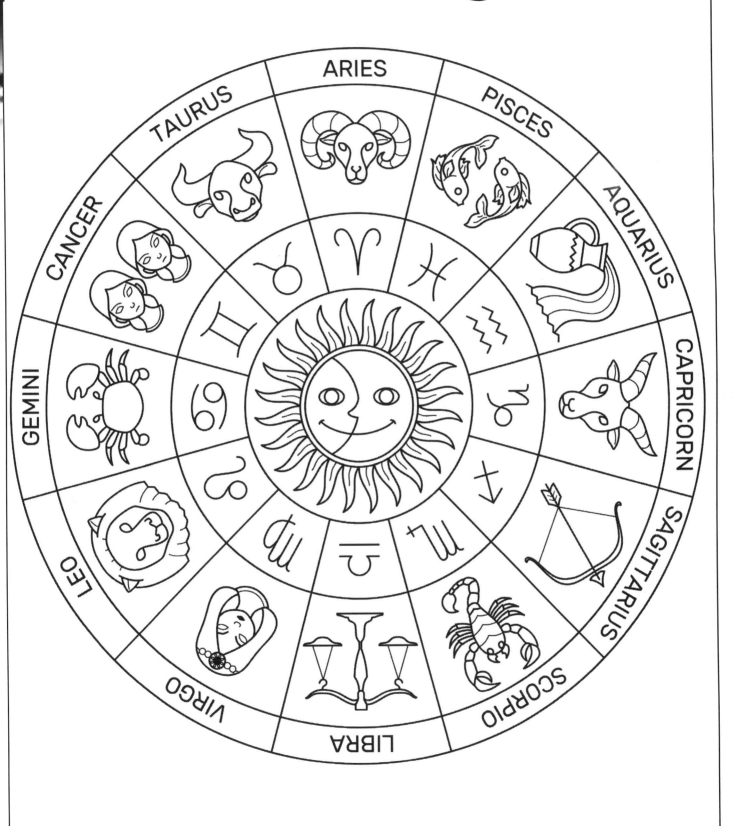

Sign Symbols

ARIES

TAURUS

GEMINI

CANCER

LEO

VIRGO

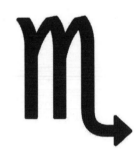

LIBRA

SCORPIO

SAGITTARIUS

CAPRICORN

AQUARIUS

PISCES

Gemini

May 21 - June 20

GEMINI, AN AIR SIGN, ruled by Mercury, the planet of communication and movement, are sociable, thoughtful, and restless. Known for their "split personality" Geminis often feel as though they are half empty and will forever search to fill that whole. Their changeable mind makes them excellent writers and artists. They are quick learners and adaptable to change. Their combination of childlike innocence and flirtatious personality make them refreshing and never boring.

Symbol: Twins

Planet: Mercury

Element: Air

Colors: Green, Yellow

Traits: Gentle, Affectionate, Adaptable, Curious, Nervous, Indecisive

Constellation:

GEMINI

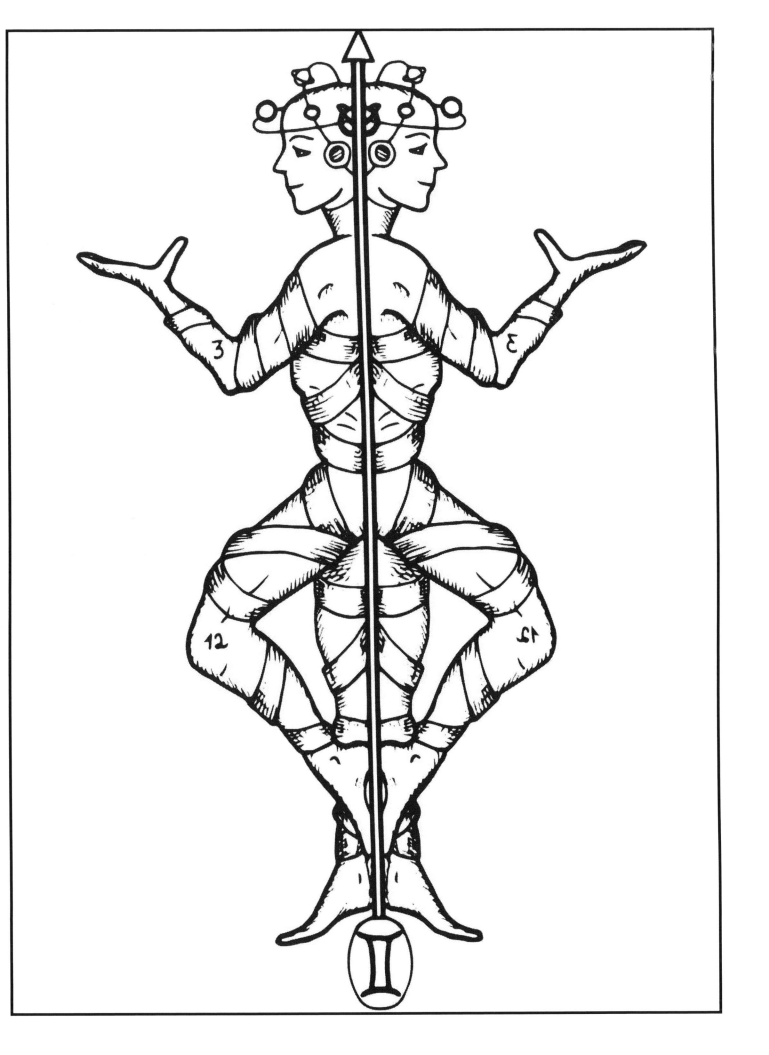

GEMINI

GEMINI

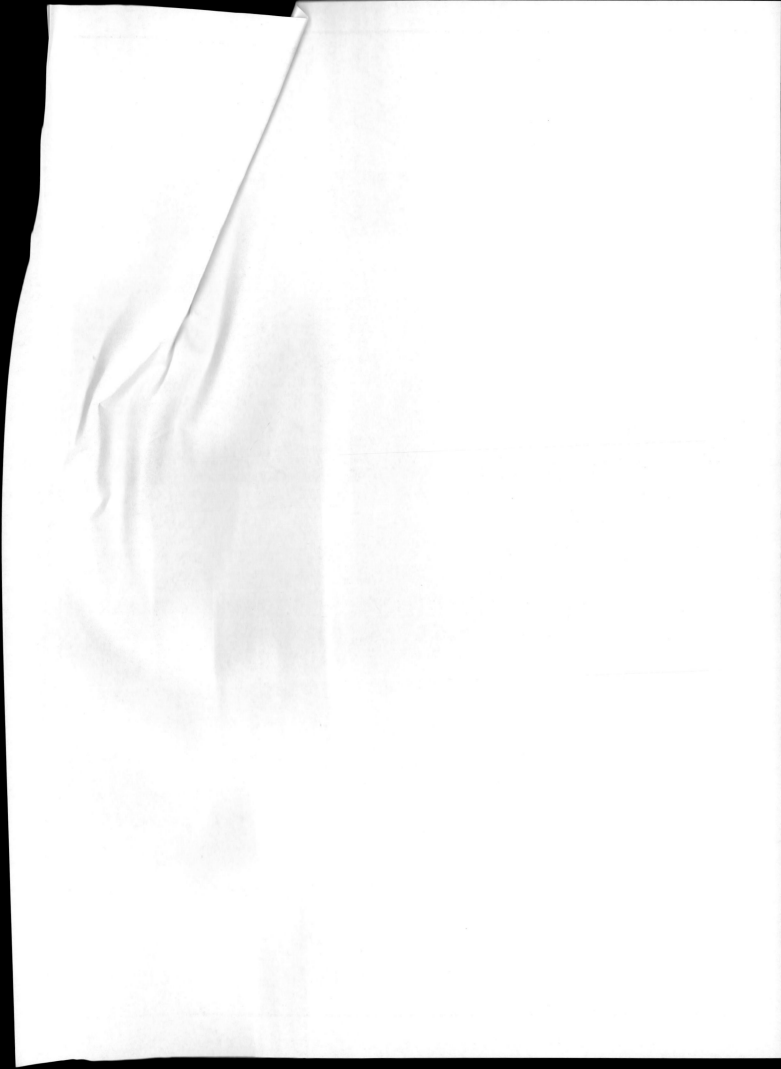

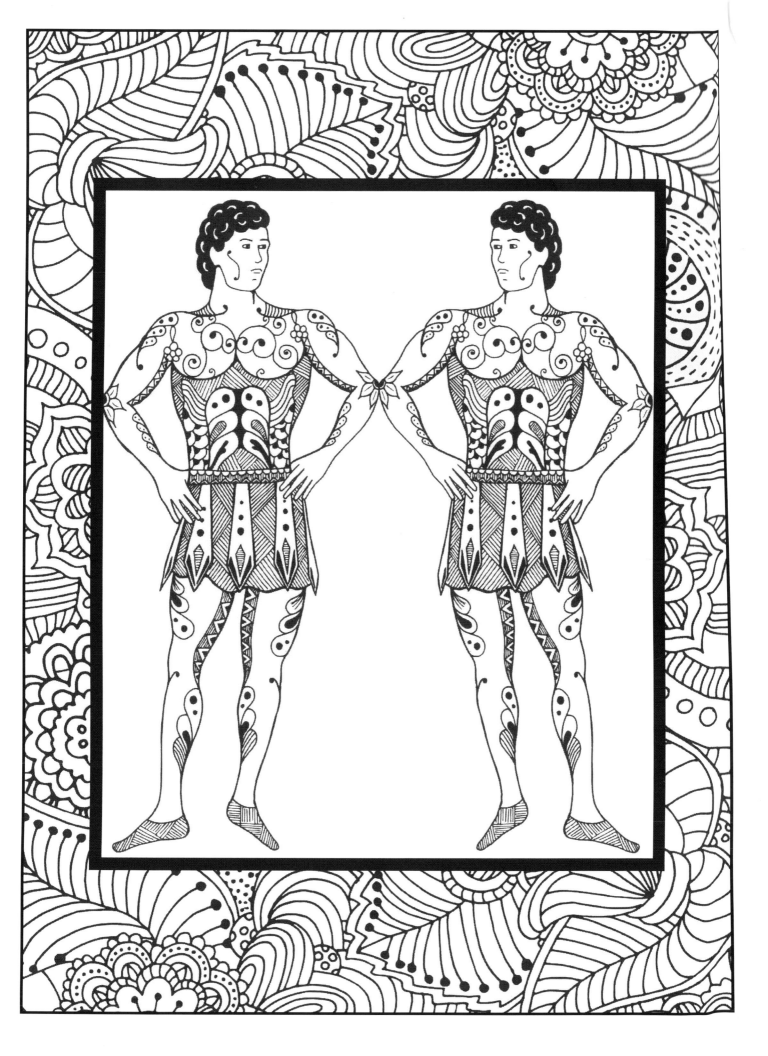

Gemini

♊ *Gemini*

Printed in Great Britain
by Amazon

15259585R00043